GramGram Plus 3

Workbook

Author Hyunjeong, Kim | **Consultant** Prof. Eunyoung, Park |
Editorial Supervisor LLS English Research Center

J PLUS
Language Publishing Co.

Can You Play Soccer?

A Write in the correct numbers and trace.

 1
 2
 3
 4
 5
 6

○ play badminton   ○ skate

○ play baseball   ○ play soccer

○ play volleyball   ○ play tennis

B Fill in the blanks to complete the cartoons.

I _____ _____ the ball.

I _____ _____ the ball, too.

But, _____ you _____ a goal, too?

No, I _____.

Oh, no!

C **Make sentences using the given hints.**

1 can't / She _____

2 can / He _____

3 can't / I _____

4 can / She _____

5 can / We _____

D **Fill in the blanks.**

My name is Jason. I really like sports.

I _____ play basketball.

When I play basketball, I _____ pass the ball.

I _____ bounce the ball, too.

However, I _____ shoot the ball well.

So, I _____ score points.

I'm going to practice every day.

E **Translate into English.**

1. 나는 자전거를 탈 수 있어.

_____

2. 나는 스케트를 탈 수 없어.

_____

A Write down the correct expressions.

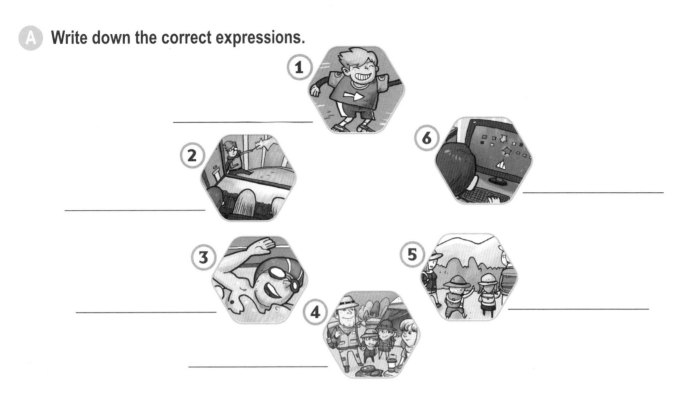

1 _____

2 _____

6 _____

3 _____

5 _____

4 _____

B Fill in the blanks to complete the cartoons.

Let's _____ _____ tomorrow.

_____ I _____ a helmet?

Yes, you _____ wear knee _____, too.

You _____ be late.

C **Write what Gram _should_ or _shouldn't_ do in each situation.**

1 Gram _____

a helmet and knee pads

2 Gram _____

a swimming hat

3 Gram _____

play computer games

4 Gram _____

stretch first

D **Fill in the blanks.**

Dear Alice,

My family will go hiking up the mountain. Let's go together.

You _____ _____ your hiking boots.

You _____ bring a hat and warm clothes, too.

My mom will cook, so you _____ prepare a lunch.

You _____ _____ to my house by 9 on Saturday.

You _____ be _____. See you on Saturday.   - Cindy.

E **Translate into English.**

1. 너는 도서관에서 조용히 해야 해. (in the library / be quiet)

_____

2. 너는 늦지 말아야 해. (be late)

_____

A Unscramble the letters.

1. u n r

_____

2. h e a c t

_____

3. y o n i s

be _____

4. f i g h t

_____

5. a t e l

be _____

6. l t i e r t

_____

B Fill in the blanks to complete the cartoons.

Please _____ me the class _____.

OK.

You _____ not be late.

ENGLISH ◎
KOREAN ✗

You _____ speak _____ English.

You must _____ be _____ in class.

C **Complete the sentences using *must* or *mustn't*.**

(**1**) You _____ follow the school rules.

(**2**) You _____ litter in school.

(**3**) You _____ use a cellphone in class.

(**4**) You _____ be quiet in class.

(**5**) You _____ fight with classmates.

(**6**) You _____ speak in English during English class.

(**7**) You _____ run in the hallway.

D **Fill in the blanks.**

I'm Mr. Henson. I will tell you three school _____.
First, you _____ _____ make fun _____ your classmates.
_____, you _____ _____ talk loudly in the library.
Third, you _____ _____ litter in school.
You must _____ trash in the trash can.
Please _____ the rules.

E **Translate into English.**

1. 학교에서는 휴대전화를 사용하면 안돼. (in school / use a cellphone)

_____

2. 수업 시간에는 조용히 해야 해. (in class / be quiet)

_____

Unit 04 You Have To Be On Time

A Fill in the blanks.

1 _____ one's mouth

2 ask to _____ the salt

3 be _____ time

4 _____ _____ one's seat

5 wait one's _____

6 _____ off one's shoes

B Fill in the blanks to complete the cartoons.

You have to _____ _____ time.

You have to eat _____.

You have to _____ with your mouth _____.

You _____ _____ ask me to _____ the salt.

C Describe each picture using *have(has) to* or *don't(doesn't) have to*.

1 → I _____

wear a dress

She _____ ←

give up one's seat

2

D Change each sentence into its question form.

1 I have to hurry. → _____

2 She has to wait her turn → _____

3 We have to be here at three o'clock. → _____

E Read and answer the questions.

NOTICE
When you get a ticket, you have to
check your seat number first.
Before the movie starts, you have
to turn off your cellphones.
You have to talk quietly during the
movie.
After the movie, you have to clean
your seat. Please bring all
of your trash to the front.
Enjoy the movie!

1. When the students get their tickets, what do they have to do?

   → _____

2. Before the movie starts, what do the students have to do?

   → _____

3. After the movie, what do the students have to do?

   → _____

F Translate into English.

1. 기침할 땐, 입을 손으로 가리고 해야 해. (cover one's mouth / when coughing)

_____

2. 너는 차례를 기다려야 해. (wait one's turn)

_____

A Write down the correct names of holidays.

| Halloween | Children's Day | New Year's Day |
| Thanksgiving | Valentine's Day | Christmas |

① _____

② _____

③ _____

④ _____

⑤ _____

⑥ _____

B Fill in the blanks to complete the cartoons.

How was your Christmas?
It _____ great!

_____ you at home?
No, I _____.

I _____ at Jason's Christmas party.

The food was _____.
It _____ a great time.

C **Change each sentence into its** past form.

1 We are excited with the party. → _____

2 My Halloween costume isn't funny. → _____

3 I am excited about the sunrise. → _____

4 Sam isn't at Ann's Christmas party. → _____

D **Look and answer the questions.**

1 Where was the boy?

_____

at the Thanksgiving party

2 How were the girls?

_____

weren't happy / with the sweaters

E **Fill in the blanks.**

Last Thursday _____ Halloween.

My sister and I _____ at a Halloween party.

The party _____ so much fun.

There was a Halloween contest.

My rabbit clothes _____ good, but I _____ the winner.

The winner _____ Susie.

F **Translate into English.**

1. 칠면조 요리는 맛있었어. (delicious / the turkey)

_____

2. 너는 선물 받고 기뻤었니? (happy / with the present)

_____

A Complete the words and match each picture with the correct words.

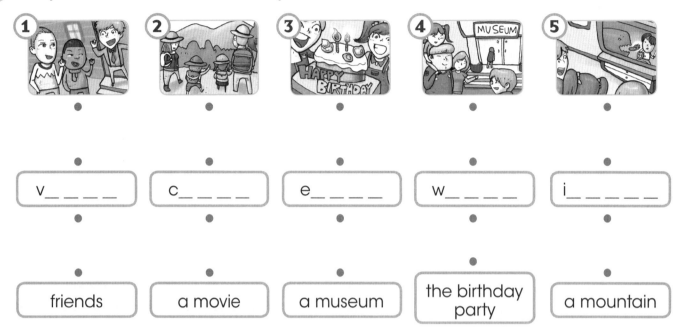

| 1 | 2 | 3 | 4 | 5 |

v_ _ _ _ _   c_ _ _ _ _   e_ _ _ _ _   w_ _ _ _ _   i_ _ _ _ _ _

friends   a movie   a museum   the birthday party   a mountain

B Fill in the blanks to complete the cartoons.

My family _____ a movie.

Then we _____ our grandparents.

We _____ about our trip to Busan.

We _____ home very late.

C Complete the chart below with verbs in the past simple form and their meaning.

Present Form	Past Form	Meaning	Present Form	Past Form	Meaning
visit			climb		
arrive			enjoy		
watch			cook		
invite			play		
wait			study		
dance			order		
like			stop		
try			talk		

D Complete each sentence with verbs in the past simple form.

(**1**) My sister _____ (like) her birthday presents.

(**2**) I _____ (plan) a trip to New York.

(**3**) Sue _____ (arrive) late yesterday.

(**4**) David _____ (play) soccer with me last Sunday.

(**5**) My brother _____ (cook) dinner for me last night.

(**6**) My family _____ (climb) a mountain today.

E Fill in the blanks.

Last Saturday was my mom's birthday.

My dad and I _____ a surprise party for her.

We _____ many balloons and _____ my mom's friends to the party.

We _____ her favorite food, too.

We _____ off the lights and _____ for her.

She really _____ the party.

F Translate into English.

1. 나는 어제 영화를 한 편 봤어. (watch a movie / yesterday)

_____

2. 나는 어젯밤에 숙제를 하지 않았어. (do one's homework / last night)

_____

We Took A Trip

A **Connect each picture with its correct expression.**

- ① go shopping
- ② take a picture
- ③ swim at the beach
- write a postcard
- buy a gift
- eat seafood
- ④
- ⑤
- ⑥

B **Fill in the blanks to complete the cartoons.**

My family _____ a trip.

We _____ at the beach.

_____ you eat seafood?

Yes, we _____.

It _____ delicious!

C Complete the chart below with verbs in the past simple form and their meaning.

Present Form	Past Form	Meaning	Present Form	Past Form	Meaning
go			meet		
get			give		
leave			say		
make			lose		
see			buy		
drink			bring		
write			have		
read			take		
come			swim		
do			eat		

D Describe each picture using the past simple form.

→ Gram _____.
　　　　　eat seafood

Gram _____. ←
　　　　　write a postcard

E Fill in the blanks.

Last summer I _____ to San Diego with my uncle.

My uncle and I _____ at the beach every day.

We _____ a boat and _____ whales in the sea.

Sometimes we _____ seafood.

We _____ shopping and _____ some gifts.

I _____ a really good time there.

F Translate into English.

1. 나는 어제 이야기 책 한 권을 읽었어. (read a story book / yesterday)

_____

2. 나는 지난 주에 Kevin을 만났어. (meet / last week)

_____

Did You Have A Good Time?

A Fill in the blanks.

1

__V st__t__on

2
a__ua__i__m

3
f__re __ta__i__n

4
a__us__me__t pa__k

5
m__s__u__

6
__ __ o

B Fill in the blanks to complete the cartoons.

_____ you take a field trip today?

Yes, I _____.

Where _____ you go?

I went to the _____.

What _____ you see?

I _____ many fish, turtles, and dolphins

_____ you have a good time?

_____, I did.

C Change each sentence into a question.

1 He saw many animals in the zoo.

→ _____?

2 She didn't go to a science museum.

→ _____?

3 You had a good time at the amusement park.

→ _____?

D Write down the proper "Wh"-question for each underlined phrase.

1 _____?

→ I met my friends at <u>4 o'clock</u>.

2 _____?

→ I went to the <u>fire station</u> for my field trip.

3 _____?

→ I <u>played baseball</u> with my friends yesterday.

E Fill in the blanks.

I went to the zoo yesterday for my field trip.

_____ did I see? I saw many interesting animals.

I liked the parrots. One parrot was _____ at singing.

What _____ I do _____ lunch?

I had a chance to _____ a horse. _____ I have a good time?

Of course! It was so _____.

F Translate into English.

1. 넌 언제 텔레비전 방송국에 갔었니? (TV station)

_____

2. Sam은 어제 영어 공부를 했었니? (study English)

_____

I Am Making Cookies

A Fill in the blanks.

1 _____ shells

2 _____ a picture

3 _____ the piano

4 _____ a picture

5 _____

6 _____ a robot

B Fill in the blanks to complete the cartoons.

_____ you _____ lunch?

No. I _____ _____.
I am _____ cookies.

But the _____ is…

It's _____ tasty.

C Complete the table below by writing the correct forms of *-ing*.

Simple Present	Present Continuous	Simple Present	Present Continuous
draw		come	
make		take	
collect		run	
write		go	
play		cook	
cut		watch	
lie		die	

D Make continuous sentences using the given hints. 'O' for the positive ones and 'X' for the negative ones.

1  → _____ .

2  → _____ .

E Fill in the blanks.

I'm Ted. I am _____ a baseball cap.

I am _____ singing. I _____ not _____ a hamburger.

I am not _____ to music.

I am not _____ a book _____ the bench.

I am not _____ basketball _____ my friends.

I am _____ a photo using a cell phone.

Who am I?

F Translate into English.

1. 난 책을 읽고 있어. (read a book)

_____

2. Sue는 기타를 치고 있지 않아. (play the guitar)

_____

Unit 10 · I Was Doing My Homework

A Connect each verb with the correct picture and phrase.

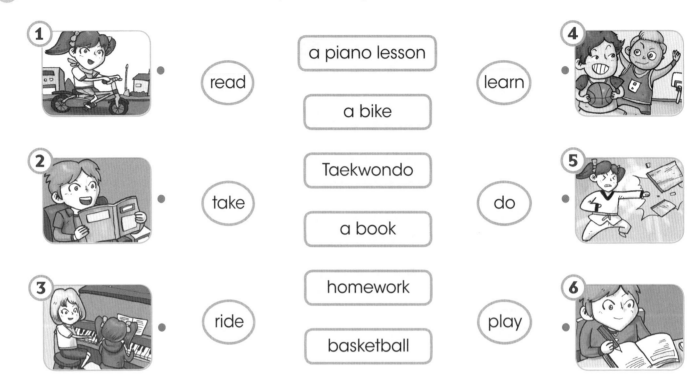

1 read
2 take
3 ride

a piano lesson
a bike
Taekwondo
a book
homework
basketball

4 learn
5 do
6 play

B Fill in the blanks to complete the cartoons.

What were you _____?
I _____ _____ my homework.

_____ were you_____?
I was _____ a book.

Wow, it's _____!
Pow

_____ were _____ doing?
I was _____ computer games.

C Complete each sentence using the past continuous.

(1) They _____ _____ books at home.

He _____ _____ learning Taekwondo. (2)

D Change each sentence into its past continuous form.

(1) John bought a book there. → _____

(2) We took an English lesson. → _____

(3) I watched a movie yesterday. → _____

(4) My sister took a walk. → _____

E Fill in the blanks.

I made a new friend today.

I _____ going to the library at 3:20.

It started to rain.

I was _____ in front of the store at 3:30.

Alex was _____ home.

He was _____ an umbrella.

We _____ _____ his umbrella with me all the way home.

F Translate into English.

1. 난 내 강아지랑 산책을 하고 있었어. (with my dog / take a walk)

_____

2. 내 남동생은 그때 음악을 듣고 있지 않았어. (then / listen to music)

_____

A Write down the correct verb for each picture.

①
_____ the dishes

②
_____ the table

③
____ _____ the trash

④
_____ the floor

⑤
_____ the room

⑥
_____ the plants

B Fill in the blanks to complete the cartoons.

C Make the correct continuous questions for each picture.

1 take out the trash

A: _____?

B: Yes, she was.

2 water the plants

A: _____?

B: Yes, he is.

D Change each sentence into its correct continuous question.

1 David vacuums the floor. → _____

2 They cleaned the room together. → _____

3 Sue does the dishes. → _____

4 My mom set the table. → _____

E Fill in the blanks.

Last Saturday was my mom's birthday.

_____ Dad _____ the floor? Yes, he was.

Was my sister washing the _____? Yes, she _____.

Was my brother cleaning _____ room? Yes, _____ was.

Was my pet _____ out the _____? Yes, he was.

Was I cleaning, _____? No, I _____.

But I was _____ dinner for my family.

We had a wonderful _____ party!

F Translate into English.

1. 너는 John과 야구를 하고 있었니? (play baseball)

_____

2. 너 지금 바이올린을 연주하고 있니? (play the violin)

_____

A Unscramble the expressions.

1.

e r t
v i e n
w i

_____

2.

w c
a
t h

_____ a movie

3.

i o
u i r s
n c g
s h n

_____ _____ the _____

4.

e i
x s e
e r c

_____

5.

p m y
l s i
u c a

_____ _____

6.

s e
t s r
a s e

_____ the _____

B Fill in the blanks to complete the cartoons.

_____ _____ you doing?

I was _____ a book.

_____ book were you _____?

Romeo And Juliet. I have a _____ meeting today.

_____?

C Write down the correct words.

(1)

A: _____ are they _____ ?

B: They are practicing _____ .

(2)

A: What _____ he doing?

B: _____ is _____ drums in the band.

D Make questions using *What* or *Where* for each underlined phrase.

(1) Q: _____ ?   A: I am <u>making cookies</u>.

(2) Q: _____ ?   A: They are going to <u>science class</u>.

(3) Q: _____ ?   A: She was reading her book <u>in her room</u>.

(4) Q: _____ ?   A: He was <u>writing for his school neswpaper</u>.

(5) Q: _____ ?   A: She is <u>singing</u> in the <u>chorus</u>.

E Fill in the blanks.

I _____ Nina _____ class. She was _____ a large box.

I asked her, "_____ are you going?"

She _____ going to her magic _____ .

We went to her club together.

Some students _____ learning magic there.

Nina told me, "_____ my club," and I did.

Then _____ _____ I doing? I was _____ MAGIC!

F Translate into English.

1. Kevin은 어디서 농구를 하고 있었니? (where / play basketball)

_____

2. 넌 무슨 음악을 듣고 있니? (what music / listen to)

_____

A Write down the correct prepositions.

> next to   under   on   in   in front of   behind

1

_____ the desk

2

_____ the closet

3

_____ the computer

4

_____ the wall

5

_____ the chair

6

_____ the desk

B Fill in the blanks to complete the cartoons.

_____ is my backpack?

It's _____ the desk.

Where _____ my English _____?

It's _____ the chair.

Where is my pencil case?

Isn't it _____ your backpack?

Oh, _____ it is.

C Describe each picture using the correct prepositions.

 **1** → The TV _____.

 **2** → The map _____.

 **3** → The cap _____.

 **4** → The box _____.

 **5** → The window _____.

D Fill in the blanks.

I have a big desk and a chair _____ my room.
The computer is _____ the _____.
The printer is _____ the _____.
The bookshelves are _____ _____ the desk.
My bed is in _____ of the _____.
Many toy boxes are _____ the bed.
My room is small but I really like it!

E Translate into English.

1. 내 여동생은 그녀의 방에 있어. (in)

_____

2. 너의 영어책이 의자 위에 있어. (on)

_____

A Fill in the blanks.

across from	movie theater	next to	post office
	and	fire station	between

1 _____ the bank

2 _____

3 _____ the bank
_____ the police station

4 _____

5 _____ the hospital

6 _____

B Fill in the blanks to complete the cartoons.

_____ is the post office?

It is ____ ____ the hospital.

_____ is the hospital?

It is _____
_____ the bank.

C Complete each sentence for each building.

1 → The bank is _____.

2 → The police station is _____.

3 → The hospital is _____.

4 → The post office is _____.

D Fill in the blanks.

Let me tell you what is around my school.

The library is _____ _____ my school.

The park is _____ _____ my school.

I ride my bike with my friends _____ the park.

Anne's Pizza is _____ the park and

the _____ _____.

We enjoy the _____ pizza there!

E Translate into English.

1. 영화관은 은행과 소방서 사이에 있어요. (between··· and···)

_____

2. 경찰서는 병원 건너편에 있어요. (across from)

_____

A Write down where each place is.

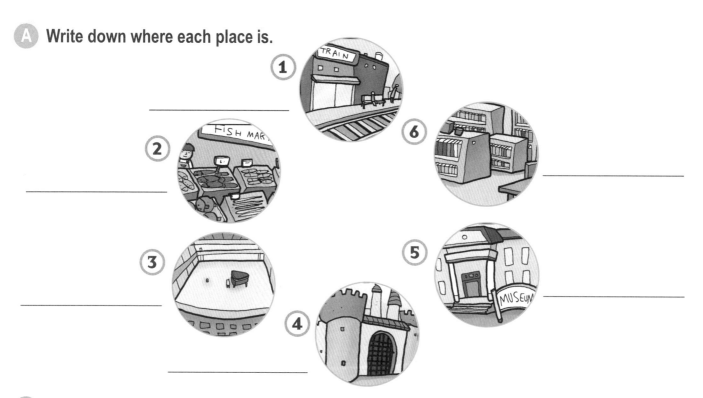

1. _____

2. _____

3. _____

4. _____

5. _____

6. _____

B Fill in the blanks to complete the cartoons.

Is _____ a zoo in your town?

Yes, there is a large _____ in my town.

_____ _____ a beautiful park _____ _____ the zoo.

_____ _____ many trees in the park?

Yes, _____ _____.

Also, _____ _____ many supermarkets in my town.

C Describe each picture using the given hints.

1. a concert hall / there is

→ _____ .

2. a fish market / my town

→ _____ .

3. many banks / my town

→ _____ .

4. many people / the library

→ _____ .

D Fill in the blanks.

My _____ place _____ town is the children's
library.

_____ are a _____ of interesting books in the library.

There _____ special _____ programs for children.

_____ _____ a small movie theater, too.

_____ _____ a garden in _____ of the library.

_____ _____ a children's library in _____ town?

E Translate into English.

1. 너희 동네에는 기차역이 있니? (there is / a train station)

_____

2. 시청 건너편에 박물관이 있어요. (a museum / across from the city hall)

_____

Unit 16 — Where Is The Bakery?

A. Connect each picture with its correct expression.

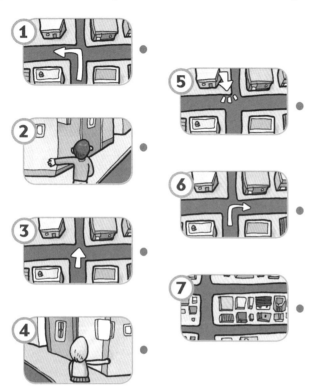

- on your right
- turn right
- go straight
- block
- at the corner
- turn left
- on your left

B. Fill in the blanks to complete the cartoons.

_____ me.
_____ is the bakery?

Bakery?

Go _____ one_____.
Then _____ right.

The _____ is
_____ your left.

C Look at the map below and write down how to get to each place starting at the star.

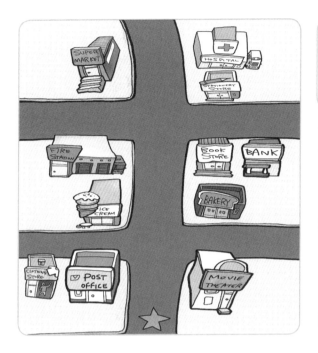

Q: Where is the hospital?
A: <u>It is next to the stationery store.</u>
   <u>Go straight three blocks. It is on your right.</u>

1 Where is the bank?

→ _____.

→ _____.

2 Where is the fire station?

→ _____.

→ _____.

3 Where is the ice cream shop?

→ _____.

→ _____.

D Fill in the blanks.

Please come to my house this Saturday
for my birthday party.
It is _____ to the stationery store.
Look at the map on this _____ card.
Start _____ the school. Go _____ one _____.
There is a bank _____ the _____.
_____ left at the corner. _____ straight.
My house is _____ your left. See you this Saturday.

E Translate into English.

1. 문구점은 어디에 있나요? (stationery store)

_____

2. 한 블록 직진해서 모퉁이에서 오른쪽으로 돌아. 병원은 네 오른쪽에 있어.
   (at the corner / the hospital / on your right)

_____

nswers

Unit 01. p.2

A.

3. play badminton   6. skate
4. play baseball   2. play soccer
5. play volleyball   1. play tennis

B.

1. I **can kick** the ball.
2. I **can pass** the ball, too.
3. But, **can** you **score** a goal, too?
4. No, I **can't**. Oh, no!

C.

1. She can't play tennis.
2. He can ride a bike.
3. I can't play soccer.
4. She can play baseball.
5. We can play badminton.

D.

My name is Jason. I really like sports.
I **can** play basketball.
When I play basketball, I **can** pass the
ball. I **can** bounce the ball, too.
However, I **can't** shoot the ball well.
So, I **can't** score points.
I'm going to practice every day.

E.

1. I can ride a bike.
2. I can't skate.

Unit 02. p.4

A.

1. in-line skate
2. go to the movies
3. go swimming
4. go camping
5. go hiking
6. play computer games

B.

1. Let's **in-line skate** tomorrow.
2. **Should** I **wear** a helmet?
3. Yes, you **should** wear knee **pads**, too.
4. You **shouldn't** be late. **OK**.

C.

1. Gram should wear a helmet and knee pads.
2. Gram should wear a swimming hat.
3. Gram shouldn't play computer games.
4. Gram should stretch first.

D.

Dear Alice,
My family will go hiking up the
mountain. Let's go together.
You **should bring** your hiking boots.
You **should** bring a hat and warm
clothes, too.
My mom will cook, so you **shouldn't**
prepare a lunch.
You **should come** to my house by 9 on
Saturday.
You **shouldn't** be **late**. See you on
Saturday. – Cindy.

E.

1. You should be quiet in the library.
2. You shouldn't be late.

Unit 03. p.6

A.

1. run   2. cheat
3. noisy   4. fight
5. late   6. litter

B.

Please **tell** me the class **rules**.
You **must** not be late.
You **must** speak **in** English.

You must **not** be **noisy** in class.

C.

1. You **must** follow the school rules.
2. You **mustn't** litter in school.
3. You **mustn't** use a cellphone in class.
4. You **must** be quiet in class.
5. You **mustn't** fight with classmates.
6. You **must** speak in English during English class.
7. You **mustn't** run in the hallway.

D.

I'm Mr. Henson. I will tell you three
school **rules**.
First, you **must not** make fun **of** your
classmates.
Second, you **must not** talk loudly in
the library.
Third, you **must not** litter in school.
You must **put** trash in the trash can.
Please **follow** the rules.

E.

1. You must not use a cellphone in school.
2. You must be quiet in class.

Unit 04. p.8

A.

1. **cover** one's mouth
2. ask to **pass** the salt
3. be **on** time
4. **give up** one's seat
5. wait one's **turn**
6. **take** off one's shoes

B.

You have to **be on** time.
You have to eat **slowly**.
You have to **chew** with your mouth **closed**.
You **have to** ask me to **pass** the salt.

C.

1. I **don't have to wear a dress**.
2. She **has to give up her seat**.

D.

1. I have to hurry. → **Do I have to hurry?**
2. She has to wait her turn. → **Does she have to wait her turn?**
3. We have to be here at three o'clock. → **Do we have to be here at three o'clock?**

E.

1. The students (They) have to check their seat numbers.
2. The students (They) have to turn off their cellphones.
3. The students (They) have to clean their seats.

F.

1. You have to cover your mouth when coughing.
2. You have to wait your turn.

Unit 05. p.10

A.

1. New Year's Day   2. Halloween
3. Children's Day   4. Christmas
5. Thanksgiving   6. Valentine's Day

B.

1. How was your Christmas? It **was** great!
2. **Were** you at home?   No, I **wasn't**.
3. I **was** at Jason's Christmas party.
4. The food was **delicious**. It **was** a great time.

C.

1. We were excited with the party.
2. My Halloween costume wasn't funny.

3. I was excited about the sunrise.
4. Sam wasn't at Ann's Christmas party.

D.

1. The boy (He) was at the Thanksgiving party.
2. The girls (They) weren't happy with the sweaters.

E.

Last Thursday **was** Halloween.
My sister and I **were** at a Halloween party.
The party **was** so much fun.
There was a Halloween contest.
My rabbit clothes **were** good, but I **wasn't** the winner.
The winner **was** Susie.

F.

1. The turkey was delicious.
2. Were you happy with the present?

Unit 06. p.12

A.

1. v **i s i t** – a museum
2. c **l i m b** - a mountain
3. e **n j o y** – the birthday party
4. w **a t c h** – a movie
5. i **n v i t e** - friends

B.

1. My family **watched** a movie.
2. Then we **visited** our grandparents.
3. We **talked** about our trip to Busan.
4. We **arrived** home very late.

C.

visit – visited – 방문하다
arrive – arrived – 도착하다
watch – watched – 지켜보다
invite – invited – 초대하다
wait – waited – 기다리다

dance – danced – 춤추다
like – liked – 좋아하다
try – tried – 노력하다
climb – climbed – 올라가다
enjoy – enjoyed – 즐기다
cook – cooked – 요리하다
play – played – 운동하다, 놀다
study – studied – 공부하다
order – ordered – 명령하다
stop – stopped – 멈추다
talk – talked – 말하다

D.

1. My sister **liked** her birthday presents.
2. I **planned** a trip to New York.
3. Sue **arrived** late yesterday.
4. David **played** soccer with me last Sunday.
5. My brother **cooked** dinner for me last night.
6. My family **climbed** a mountain today.

E.

Last Saturday was my mom's birthday.
My dad and I **planned** a surprise party for her.
We **prepared** many balloons and **invited** my mom's friends to the party.
We **cooked** her favorite food, too.
We **turned** off the lights and **waited** for her.
She really **liked** the party.

F.

1. I watched a movie yesterday.
2. I didn't do my homework last night.

Unit 07. p.14

A.

1. eat seafood
2. buy a gift
3. write a postcard

Answers

4. go shopping
5. take a picture
6. swim at the beach

B.

1. My family **took** a trip.
2. We **swam** at the beach.
3. **Did** you eat **seafood**? Yes, we **did**.
4. It **was** delicious!

C.

go – went – 가다
get – got – 얻다
leave – left – 떠나다
make – made – 만들다
see – saw – 보다
drink – drank – 마시다
write – wrote – 쓰다
read – read – 읽다
come – came – 오다
do – did – 하다
meet – met – 만나다
give – gave – 주다
say – said – 말하다
lose – lost – 잃다
buy – bought – 사다
bring – brought – 가져오다
have – had – 가지다
take – took – 가지고 가다
swim – swam – 수영하다
eat – ate – 먹다

D.

1. Gram **ate seafood**.
2. Gram **wrote a postcard**.

E.

Last summer I **went** to San Diego with my uncle.
My uncle and I **swam** at the beach every day.
We **took** a boat and **saw** whales in the

sea.
Sometimes we **ate** seafood.
We **went** shopping and **bought** some gifts.
I **had** a really good time there.

F.

1. I read a story book yesterday.
2. I met Kevin last week.

Unit 08. p.16

A.

1. **T**V st**ati**on
2. a**q**u**a**ri**u**m
3. f**i**re st**ati**on
4. a**m**us**e**men**t** par**k**
5. m**use**um
6. **zo**o

B.

1. **Did** you take a field trip today?
   Yes, I **did**.
2. Where **did** you go?
   I went to the **aquarium**.
3. What **did** you see?
   I **saw** many fish, turtles, and dolphins.
4. **Did** you have a good time?
   Yes, I did.

C.

1. Did he see many animals in the zoo?
2. Didn't she go to a science museum?
3. Did you have a good time in the amusement park?

D.

1. When did you meet your friends?
2. Where did you go for your field trip?
3. What did you do yesterday?

E.

I went to the zoo yesterday for my field trip.
What did I see? I saw many interesting animals.
I liked the parrots. One parrot was **good** at singing.
What **did** I do **after** lunch?
I had a chance to **feed** a horse.
Did I have a good time?
Of course! It was so **exciting**.

F.

1. When did you go to the TV station?
2. Did Sam study English yesterday?

Unit 09. p.18

A.

1. **collect** shells   2. **take** a picture
3. **play** the piano   4. **draw** a picture
5. **swim**   6. **make** a robot

B.

1. **Are** you **eating** lunch?
2. No. I **am cooking**. I am **making** cookies.
3. But the **problem** is…
4. It's **not** tasty.

C.

draw – drawing
make – making
collect – collecting
write – writing
swim – swimming
cut – cutting
lie – lying
come – coming
take – taking
run – running
go – going
read – reading

watch – watching

die – dying

D.

1. She is playing the piano.
2. He is not taking a photo.

E.

I'm Ted. I am **wearing** a baseball cap.
I am **not** singing. I **am** not **eating** a hamburger.
I am not **listening** to music.
I am not **reading** a book **on** the bench.
I am not **playing** basketball **with** my friends.
I am **taking** a photo using a cell phone.
Who am I?

F.

1. I am reading a book.
2. Sue is not playing the guitar.

Unit 10 p.20

A.

1. ride – a bike
2. read – a book
3. take – a piano lesson
4. play – basketball
5. learn – Taekwondo
6. do - homework

B.

1. What were you **doing**?
   I **was doing** my homework.
2. **What** were you **doing**?
   I was **reading** a book.
3. Wow, it's **fun**!
4. **What** were **you** doing?
   I was **playing** computer games.

C.

1. They **were reading** books at home.
2. He **was** **not** learning Taekwondo.

D.

1. John was buying a book there.
2. We were taking an English lesson.
3. I was watching a movie yesterday.
4. My sister was taking a walk.

E.

I made a new friend today.
I **was** going to the library at 3:20.
It started to rain.
I was **standing** in front of the store at 3:30.
Alex was **going** home.
He was **holding** an umbrella.
We **were sharing** his umbrella with me all the way home.

F.

1. I was taking a walk with my dog.
2. My brother was not listening to music then.

Unit 11 p.22

A.

1. **do** the dishes
2. **set** the table
3. **take** out the trash
4. **vacuum** the floor
5. **clean** the room
6. **water** the plants

B.

1. **Are** you **cleaning** your room?
   Yes, I am.
2. Gram, **are** you **in** your room?
3. No, I am in the **yard**.
4. Are you **watering** the plants?
   Of course, **I am**.

C.

1. Was she taking out the trash?
2. Is he watering the plants?

D.

1. Is David vacuuming the floor?
2. Were they cleaning the room together?
3. Is Sue doing the dishes?
4. Was my mom setting the table?

E.

Last Saturday was my mom's birthday.
Was Dad **vacuuming** the floor? Yes, he was.
Was my sister washing the **dishes**? Yes, she **was**.
Was my brother cleaning **his** room? Yes, **he** was.
Was my pet **taking** out the **trash**? Yes, he was.
Was I cleaning, **too**? No, I **wasn't**.
But I was **cooking** dinner for my family.
We had a wonderful **birthday** party!

F.

1. Were you and John playing baseball?
2. Are you playing the violin now?

Unit 12 p.24

A.

1. **interview**
2. **watch** a movie
3. **sing in** the **chorus**
4. **exercise**
5. **play music**
6. **see** the **stars**

B.

1. **What were** you doing?
   I was **reading** a book.
2. **What** book were you **reading**?
3. Romeo And Juliet. I have a **club**

Answers

meeting today.
4. **Really**?

C.

1. A: **What** are they **doing**?
   B: They are practicing **English**.
2. A: What **is** he doing?
   B: **He** is **playing** drums in the band.

D.

1. What are you doing?
2. Where are they going?
3. Where was she reading her book?
4. What was he doing?
5. What is she doing?

E.

I **met** Nina **after** class.
She was **holding** a large box.
I asked her, "**Where** are you going?"
She **was** going to her magic **club**.
We went to her club together.
Some students **were** learning magic
there.
Nina told me, "**Join** my club," and I did.
Then **what was** I doing?
I was **learning** MAGIC!

F.

1. Where was Kevin playing basketball?
2. What music are you listening to?

Unit 13 p.26

A.

1. **behind** the desk
2. **in** the closet
3. **in front of** the computer
4. **on** the wall
5. **under** the chair
6. **next to** the desk

B.

1. **Where** is my backpack?
   It's **under** the desk.
2. Where **is** my English **book**?
   It's **on** the chair.
3. Where is my pencil case?
   Isn't it **in** your **backpack**?
4. Oh, **here** it is.

C.

1. The TV **is in front of the window**.
2. The map **is on the wall**.
3. The cap **is under the bed**.
4. The box **is in the closet**.
5. The window **is behind the desk**.

D.

I have a big desk and a chair **in** my
room.
The computer is **on** the **desk**.
The printer is **behind** the **computer**.
The bookshelves are **next to** the desk.
My bed is in **front** of the **window**.
Many toy boxes are **under** the bed.
My room is small but I really like it!

E.

1. My sister is in her room.
2. Your English book is on the chair.

Unit 14 p.28

A.

1. **next to** the bank
2. **movie theater**
3. **between** the bank **and** the police
   station
4. **fire station**
5. **across from** the hospital
6. **post office**

B.

1. **Where** is the post office?
2. It is **next to** the hospital.
3. **Where** is the hospital?
4. It is **across from** the bank.

C.

1. The bank is **next to the hospital**.
2. The police station is **across from the park**.
3. The hospital is **between the park and the bank**.
4. The post office is **next to the bank**.

D.

Let me tell you what is around my
school.
The library is **next to** my school.
The park is **across from** my school.
I ride my bike with my friends **in** the
park.
Anne's Pizza is **between** the park and
the **post office**.
We enjoy the **delicious** pizza there!

E.

1. The movie theater is between the
   bank and the fire station.
2. The police station is across from the
   hospital.

Unit 15 p.30

A.

1. train station   2. fish market
3. concert hall   4. old palace
5. museum   6. library

B.

1. Is **there** a zoo in your town?
   Yes, there is a large **zoo** in my town.
2. **There is** a beautiful park **next to** the
   zoo.

3. **Are** **there** many trees in the park?
Yes, **there** **are**.

4. Also, **there** **are** many supermarkets in my town.

C.

1. There is a concert hall next to the park.
2. There is a fish market in my town.
3. There are many banks in my town.
4. There are many people in the library.

D.

My **favorite** place **in** town is the children's library.

There are a **lot** of interesting books in the library.

There **are** special **reading** programs for children.

There is a small movie theater, too.

There is a garden in **front** of the library.

Is there a children's library in **your** town?

E.

1. Is there a train station in your town?
2. There is a museum across from the city hall.

Unit 16 p.32

A.

1 – turn left

2 – on your left

3 – go straight

4 – on your right

5 – at the corner

6 – turn right

7 – block

B.

1. **Excuse** me. **Where** is the bakery?

Bakery?

2. Go **straight** one **block**. Then **turn** right.

3. The **bakery** is **on** your left.

C.

1. It is next to the bookstore.
Go straight two blocks and turn right.
It is on your right.

2. It is across from the supermarket.
Go straight two blocks and turn left.
It's on your left.

3. It is across from the post office.
Go straight one block and turn left.
It's on your right.

D.

Please come to my house this Saturday for my birthday party.

It is **next** to the stationery store.

Look at the map on this **invitation** card.

Start **at** the school. Go **straight** one **block**.

There is a bank **at** the **corner**.

Turn left at the corner. **Go** straight.

My house is **on** your left.

See you this Saturday.

E.

1. Where is the stationery store?
2. Go straight one block and turn right at the corner. The hospital is on your right.

GramGram Plus 3
Workbook

First Printing 2014.3.20

Author Hyunjeong, Kim

Consultant Prof. Eunyoung, Park

Editorial Supervisor LLS English Research Center

Publisher Kiseon, Lee

Publishing Company JPLUS

62, World Cup-ro 31-gil, Mapo-gu, Seoul, Korea

Telephone 02-332-8320

Fax 02-332-8321

Homepage www.jplus114.com

Registration Number 10-1680

Registration Date 1998.12.09

ISBN 979-11-5601-018-0(64740)